HOLISTIC
PLAN OF CARE

MENTAL HEALTH WORKBOOK

Dr. Barbara Thomas-Reddick, PhD, CAP

To order additional copies of this book, contact:
Xlibris
844-714-8691
www.Xlibris.com
Orders@Xlibris.com

ISBN: Softcover   979-8-3694-0219-1
           EBook   979-8-3694-0218-4

Print information available on the last page

Rev. date: 06/29/2023

Mental Health: Mental health includes our emotional, psychological, and social well-being. It affects how we think, feel, and act. It also helps determine how we handle stress, relate to others, and make healthy choices. Mental health is important at every stage of life, from childhood and adolescence through adulthood.

Mental health is important because it can help you to:

- Cope with the stresses of life.
- Be physically healthy.
- Have good relationships.
- Make meaningful contributions to your community.
- Work productively.
- Realize your full potential.

Cope with stresses of life

Name one stressor you are dealing with currently.

_____

_____

_____

_____

Name and explain what it is:

_____

_____

_____

_____

_____

_____

_____

_____

Explain how you are coping with it:

_____

_____

_____

_____

Is it someone you are angry with? If it is, how are you trying to make amends with this individual? Do you want to make amends with this person? If not, why not?

_____

_____

_____

_____

_____

_____

_____

_____

_____

BE PHYSICALLY HEALTHY

When was the last time you had a wells checkup?
_____this year _____last year _____ two years ago _____don't know.

If you haven't had a check up in a while, stop and consider scheduling a checkup with your primary care doctor. If you do not have one, try to find a doctor you feel comfortable with.

Write down the doctor you chose: _____
(THIS WILL BE A PART OF YOUR EXIT)

GREAT JOB FOR SCHEDULING YOUR DOCTOR'S APPOINTMENT!!!!!

HAVE GOOD RELATIONSHIPS

RESPECT***********TRUST***************AFFECTION

Respect in the relationship means that you both hold each other in high regard. When you respect someone, you admire them for certain qualities they possess and/or the character they embody.

Trust in each other means you take each other at your word. If one person says they're going to do something, the other person assumes they'll do as they say. If someone makes a mistake, the other person expects them to be honest and tell them. In fact, just comes down to each person being completely honest with the other, even when it's uncomfortable.

Affection in healthy relationships is freely given and received. Healthy couples don't need to remind themselves to show their partner that they love and appreciate them. They just do.

MAKING MEANINGFUL CONTRIBUTIONS TO YOUR COMMUNITY

In the past, identify ways you have contributed to the community.

1._____

2._____

3._____

Moving forward, identify ways you intend to contribute to the community.

1._____

2._____

3._____

4._____

Do you feel you have something to contribute to the community. If so, write them down.

1._____

2._____

3._____

Work productively

Are you working productively:
a. Yes _____ Explain how you are working productively?

_____

_____

b. No _____ What is keeping you from working productively?

_____

_____

REALIZE YOUR FULL POTENTIAL

What do you intend to achieve in life?

_____

_____

Explain your plan for reaching this achievement?

_____

_____

How can our Holistic Plan of Care Team help you achieve your goal(s)?

_____

_____

POWERFUL QUOTE FOR MENTAL HEALTH

"Being able to look at yourself in the mirror and identifying who you are is one of the strongest components of good mental health." All stress, anxiety, and depression are caused when we ignore who we are, and start living to please others. To maintain wellbeing, individuals need to recognize their inner strengths."

Short Mental Health Quotes

What we think, we become--------Buddha

All limitations are self-imposed------Oliver Wendall Holmes

Tough times never last but tough people do--------Robert H. Schuller

What consumes your mind controls your life-------Unknown

And still, I rise-------Maya Angelou

Turn your wounds into wisdom-------------Oprah Winfrey

Persist and resist-----Epictetus

Change what you can, manage what you can't----Raymond McCauley

If you're going through hell, keep going -------Winston Churchill

Self-care is how you take your power back.—Lalah Delia

Mental Health Assessment

1. Moving or speaking so slowly that it is noticeable to others or could have noticed. Even being so fidgety or restless that you have been moving around a lot more than usual.
    a. not at all _____
    b. Some days _____
    c. Majority of the day _____
    d. Nearly every day _____

2. Thoughts that no one cares for you, or you would be better off dead, or of self-mutilation/hurting yourself.
    a. not at all _____
    b. Some days _____
    c. Majority of the day _____
    d. Nearly every day _____

3. Feeling down depressed, without, empty, or hopeless
    a. not at all _____
    b. Some days _____
    c. Majority of the day _____
    d. Nearly every day _____

4. Trouble falling or staying asleep or sleeping too much.
    Poor appetite or overeating
    a. not at all _____
    b. Some days _____
    c. Majority of the day_____
    d. Nearly every day _____

5. Feeling bad about yourself or that you are a failure or have let yourself or your family down.
    a. not at all _____
    b. Some days _____
    c. Majority of the day _____
    d. Nearly every day _____

6. Trouble concentrating on things such as reading the newspaper or watching the telephone.
    a. not at all _____
    b. Some days _____
    c. Majority of the day _____
    d. Nearly every day _____

    Total Not at all _____
    Total Several Days _____
    Total Majority of the day _____
    Total Nearly every day _____

7. In the past week, I felt happier or more cheerful than usual.
    a. Not at all
    b. Often
    c. Very Often
    d. Regularly
    e. All the time

8. In the past week, I have been more active than usual (either socially, sexually, at work, home, or school).
    a. Not at all
    b. Often
    c. Very Often
    d. Regularly
    e. All the time

9. Repeated, disturbing, and unwanted memories of the stressful experience?
   a. Not at all
   b. Somewhat
   c. Fairly
   d. Satisfactorily Much
   e. Majority of the time

10. Suddenly feeling or acting as if the stressful experience were happening again (as if you were back there reliving it)?
    a. Not at all
    b. Somewhat
    c. Fairly
    d. Satisfactorily Much
    e. Majority of the time

11. Feeling very upset when something reminds you of a stressful experience?

    a. Not at all
    b. Somewhat
    c. Fairly
    d. Satisfactorily Much
    e. Majority of the time

12. Having strong physical reactions when something reminds you of a stressful experience (for example, heart pounding, trouble breathing, sweating)?
    a. Not at all
    b. Somewhat
    c. Fairly
    d. Satisfactorily Much
    e. Majority of the time

13. Having strong negative beliefs about yourself, other people, or the world.
    a. Not at all
    b. Sometimes
    c. A Lot

14. Have any of your closest relationships been troubled by a lot of arguments or repeated breakups. (Check yes or no)
    a. Yes _____
    b. No _____

15. Have you deliberately hurt yourself physically (e.g., punched yourself, cut yourself, burned yourself)? How about making a suicide attempt? (Check yes or no)
    a. Yes _____
    b. No _____

16. Have you been extremely moody? (Check yes or no)
    a. Yes _____
    b. No _____

17. Have you felt very angry a lot of the time? How about often acting in an angry or sarcastic manner? (Check yes or no)
    a. Yes _____
    b. No _____

18. Recently, have there been times you were distrustful of others, more often than other times? (Check yes or no)
    a. Yes _____
    b. No _____

19. Lately have things seemed unreal or you felt unreal or numb? (Check yes or no)
    a. Yes _____
    b. No _____

20. Have you felt empty or like a strong void in your life? (Check yes or no)
    a. Yes _____
    b. No _____

21. Have there been times you had to wonder, "Who Am I"? (Check yes or no)
    a. Yes _____
    b. No _____

22. Have you found yourself talking to yourself? (Check yes or no)
    a. Yes _____
    b. No _____

23. Has others looked at you strange and you wondered what in the world
    are they looking at me for? (Check yes or no)
    a. Yes _____
    b. No _____

24. Do you feel that nobody loves you? (Check yes or no)
    a. Yes _____
    b. No _____

25. How do you feel about animals?
    a. Don't care about them.
    b. They are okay.
    c. Love them.
    d. Don't really know.

26. Who are you closest to? (Circle)

Mother	Father	Sister	Brother
Auntie	Uncle	Grandmother	Grandfather
Cousin	Friend	Pastor	Mentor
Counselor	Classmate	Teacher	Professor
Neighbor	Nobody	Boyfriend	Girlfriend
Stepmother	Stepfather	Need to thank about it	Not Sure
Comments:			

Anger management:

The goal of anger management is to minimize both your feelings and emotions, the physiological awakening that anger causes. You can't get rid of, or avoid, the things or the people that antagonize you, nor can you change them, but you can learn to control your reactions. Our hope is that you learn the necessary coping skills that you need to journey in a positive direction and to maintain, sustain and manage your anger. You will learn the three types of Anger: **Passive Aggression, Open Aggression, and Assertive Aggression**. We will talk about the five stages of Anger: **Trigger, Escalation, Crisis, Recovery, and Depression. Before discussing the three types of Anger, lets assess our FEELINGS.**

Learning to recognize and express anger appropriately can make a bid difference in your life.

FEELINGS CHECK: Simply identify your feelings at this time and write it here: _____

FEELINGS CHECK-IN

Excited

Happy

Surprised

Angry

Sad

Scared

Nervous

Hurt

Proud

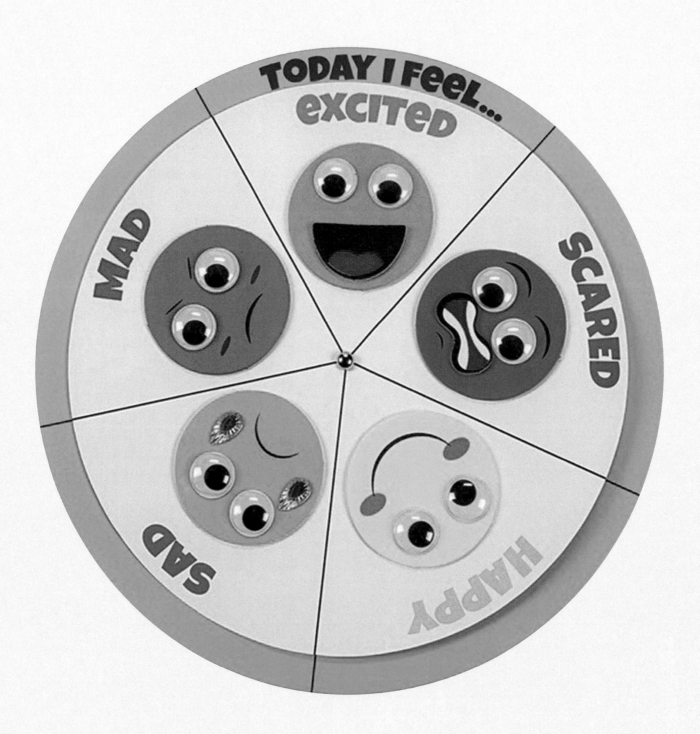

If you identify more than one identify them here:

1.	2.	3.		
4.	5.	6.		

Take each one of the feelings you have identified and discuss what those feelings means to you.

Your Feelings:

_____

Why are you feeling this way?

_____

_____

What cause you to feel this way?

_____

_____

_____

What are you doing to change this feeling?

_____

_____

_____

Are you Angry?

_____

_____

_____

If you are Angry, do you know Who you are Angry with?

_____

_____

_____

_____

How do you want to resolve this matter?

_____

_____

_____

_____

If there is someone you need to make amends, do you want to make amends?

_____

_____

_____

_____

_____

If no, why not?

_____

_____

_____

If you need to make amends, skip to page 29-32 and then return back to this page after you complete "Making Amends" assignment.

_____

_____

_____

_____

_____

(PRE) TESTING YOUR ANGER CONTROL

1. I get angry with little or no provocation.

   1   2   3   4   5

2. I have a really bad temper.

   1   2   3   4   5

3. It's hard for me to let go of thoughts that make me angry.

   1   2   3   4   5

4. When I become angry, I have urges to beat someone up.

   1   2   3   4   5

5. When I become angry, I have urges to break or tear things.

   1   2   3   4   5

6. I get impatient when people don't understand me.

   1   2   3   4   5

7. I lose my temper at least once a week.

   1   2   3   4   5

8. I embarrass family, friends, or coworkers with my anger outbursts.

   1   2   3   4   5

9. I get impatient when people in front of me drive *exactly at* the speed limit.

   1   2   3   4   5

10. When my neighbors are inconsiderate, it makes me angry.

    1   2   3   4   5

11. I find myself frequently annoyed with certain friends or family.

    1   2   3   4   5

12. I get angry when people do things that they are not supposed to, like smoking in a no smoking section or having more items than marked in the supermarket express checkout line.

    1   2   3   4   5

13. There are certain people who always rub me the wrong way.

    1   2   3   4   5

14. I feel uptight/tense.

    1   2   3   4   5

15. I yell and/or curse.

    1   2   3   4   5

16. I get so angry I feel like I am going to explode with rage.

    1   2   3   4   5

17. I get easily frustrated when machines/equipment do not work properly

    1   2   3   4   5

18. I remember people and situations that made me angry for a long time.

    1   2   3   4   5

19. I can't tolerate incompetence. It makes me angry.

    1   2   3   4   5

20. I think people try to take advantage of me.

    1   2   3   4   5

TOTAL: _____

Score Key:

80-100 Your anger expression is likely getting you into serious trouble with others. It would probably be worthwhile to seek professional help.

60-80 You may not need professional help but you need to work on controlling your anger in a very deliberate manner.

50-60 You have plenty of room for improvement. Reading a self help book on anger control could be beneficial.

30-50 You're probably getting angry as often as most people. Monitor your episodes of temper and see if you can lower your score in this test in 6 months.

Below 30- Congratulate yourself. You are likely in a good comfort zone.

Passive Aggression, Open Aggression, and Assertive Aggression.
Now let's discuss the three types of Anger.

- ## Passive Aggressive

  Passive-aggressive behavior is when one person is subtly aggressive towards another. This behavior aims to punish or retaliate to a perceived slight. A person exhibiting this behavior will use passive-aggressive actions rather than communicating their dissatisfaction with words. When you have been the target of this behavior, you may not realize that a person's hostility was purposeful. You may be left wondering why the person treated you poorly. Was it an accident? Are you being too sensitive?

- ## What are some of the reason people? behave passively aggressively?

  1. Most of the time individuals use passive-aggressive behavior for different reasons. A person may not typically behave this way, but occasionally they will exhibit this behavior. According to clinical studies, Dr. B. Thomas Reddick, there are reasons why people act this way.

     - We are taught showing anger is intolerable.
     - Cover up or sugarcoated angry responses are welcome.
     - Aggressiveness is harder.
     - Trouble Free to rationalize behavior.
     - Getting Even feels superior.
     - Advantageous
     - Feel effective

• Examples of Passive-Aggressive Behavior

Stubbornness, procrastination, and a get back behavior are typically exhibited. A person may false-face their anger by making excuses for their non-receptiveness. People who are confrontational or aggressive may deny being angry even though it is obvious that they are upset. A procrastinating passive-aggressive co-worker may wait until the last minute to complete their assigned work or submit work late as a means of getting back.

• Passive Aggressive Speech

There are common ways that people speak to show their hidden unkindness. You may notice that the way they are talking to you doesn't quite make sense and that you are getting frustrated. According to clinical studies, passive-aggressive people may say:

- o "I'm okay."
- o "I'm not angry."
- o "Okay"
- o "Anyway"
- o "I thought you knew."
- o "I'd be delighted to."
- o "I was only playing."
- o "Why are you mad?"

• Open Aggressive

Open aggression is a sharp contrast to passive-aggressive anger, as it's usually expressed outwardly---- mostly in a physically or verbally aggressive way. People who express outward anger often do so with the of hurting others or destroying things to retaliate for acts they perceived were wrongfully done to them.

Many people tend to lash out in anger and rage, becoming physically or verbally aggressive and can often times hurt themselves or others. Open Aggression comes out in bullying, blackmailing, accusing, shouting, bickering, sarcasm, fighting, and criticism.

How to control your anger
1. Count to 10. Counting to 10 gives you time to cool down, so you can think more clearly and overcome the impulse to lash out.
2. Breathe slowly. ...
3. Inhale and Exhale
4. Exercise can help with anger. ...
5. Looking after yourself may keep you calm. ...
6. Get creative. ...
7. Talk about how you feel. ...
8. Anger management programs.
9. Méditation/Yoga/Payer/Read a Book etc.

• **Assertive Agressive**

Assertive anger: This is usually the best way to communicate feelings of anger because anger is expressed directly and in a nonthreatening way to the person involved. A statement such as "I feel angry when you ..." is an example of assertive anger.

We will talk about the five stages of Anger: **Trigger, Escalation, Crisis, Recovery, and Depression.**

Trigger:

Everyone has their own triggers for what makes them angry, but some common ones include situations in which we feel:

- Threatened or attacked.
- Frustrated or powerless
- Like we're being invalidated or treated unfairly
- Like people are not respecting our feelings or possessions.

Start by considering these 10 anger management tips.
a. Think before you speak.
b. Once you're calm, express your concerns.
c. Get some exercise.
d. Identify possible solutions.
e. Stick with "I" statements.
f. Don't hold a grudge.
g. Use humor to release tension.

Escalation:

Escalation. In this process, the escalation phase involves cues that indicate anger is building. As stated in the introduction to anger management, these cues can be physical, behavioral, emotional, or cognitive (thoughts). As you may recall, cues are warning signs, or responses, to anger-provoking events.

The Four-Step Verbal De-Escalation Process
- Step 1: Recognize and Assess the Situation. Your safety is paramount. ...
- Step 2: Respond Calmly. Human beings tend to mimic each other's behavior, so don't respond with anger, sarcasm, or inflexibility. ...
- Step 3: Listen with Empathy. ...
- Step 4: Validate and Show Respect.

Crisis:

The crisis phase involves the young person behaving in an aggressive manner, either physically or verbally, towards another person, an object or themselves. This may include shouting, throwing, or hitting an object and or striking a person.

Recovery:

Recovery is the physiological and psychological winddown phase that returns a young person to a pre-angry state. This slow cool down process can take from less than an hour to days, depending on the intensity and length of the anger-related episode.

Depression:

People with depressive illness often have symptoms of overt or suppressed anger. Can depression make you have anger issues?

Those with anger traits face exaggerated problems during symptomatic period of depression. Pharmacological management helps in control of depressive and anxiety symptoms, but rarely addresses anger symptoms.

Dealing with someone else's Anger:

Here are some tips:

Keep your cool. Don't answer anger with anger. Remember that anger can lead people to say things they don't really mean. Criticism, threats, or name-calling won't help resolve the situation. Don't take it personally. Try to understand why the person is angry. His or her feelings may have little or nothing to do with you. Listen to the person. Sometimes an angry person just needs to "blow off steam". Let the person express his or her feelings. Don't interrupt. Maintain eye contact to show you are listening. Think of solutions together. If you're having a conflict with someone, try to find solutions that you can both agree on. Do this only when you are both calm.

Some Common causes of anger to include, but not limited to:

1. **Stress:** Stress related to work, family, health, and money problems may make you feel anxious and irritable.

2. **Frustration/Resentment**: You may get angry if you fail to reach a goal or feel as if things are out of your control.

3. **Anxiety/Fear:** Anger is a natural response to threats of violence or to physical or verbal abuse.

4. **Aggravation/Annoyance:** You may reach in anger to minor irritations and daily hassles.

5. **Sadness/Disappointment:** Anger often results when expectations and desires aren't met.

6. **Bitterness/Resentment:** You may feel angry when you've been hurt, rejected, or offended.

MAKING AMENDS

Credit to Nick https://www.amethystrecovery.org

As to Nick writing with Amethyst recovery & Dr. B. Thomas-Reddick believes that MAKING AMENDS is a vital part of an individual's life. When one understands the proper steps in how to make amends with people, they have either hurt or caused discomfort too, this allows one to fill the voids. Studies has proven that when an individual suffers with addictions one of the 12 steps that every Alcoholic Anonymous or Drug Disorder member needs to complete is rekindling with loved ones, family and friends. Not only does making amends help you get over past mistakes, but it also helps repair your relationships with other people. However, some people are afraid of making amends because they don't know what to say, how to start, or how others are going to respond. While everyone's journey is different, and you cannot control how others will respond, there are ways to approach this step appropriately.

Start With a Thoughtful Apology

When you make amends, you must apologize for the hurt and pain you caused. Keep in mind, it doesn't have to be a lengthy apology; it just needs to be honest. Some things you can open with include:

- I'm sorry.
- I feel bad about what I did.
- I'm sorry I made myself sick.

- I'm sorry for what I've put you through.
- I know this has been hard on both of us.

Take Responsibility for Your Actions

Don't deny responsibility for the harm you've caused, even if you think it was someone else's fault or the victim brought it to themselves. When making amends, owning the responsibility for your actions can sound like:

- I recognize I am powerless against drinking, or I recognize I am powerless against drugs.
- I accept responsibility for what I did.
- I know that I caused you harm.
- I acknowledge that I ignored your help.
- I realize that my actions were hurtful.

Admit What You Did Wrong

One of the most important parts of making amends is being specific about what you did wrong. Rather than saying something vague like, "I'm sorry for being rude to you," say something like, "When you were trying to introduce yourself at that party, I interrupted and made inappropriate comments, and I apologize for my behavior. Please accept my apology."

Don't try to justify what happened either; simply admit that your actions were wrong without explaining why they occurred in the first place. One way to recognize what you did wrong is by saying things like:

- I was wrong.
- I did this and I take full responsibility for my actions.
- This was my fault.

Genuinely Feel Remorse

It is important to genuinely feel remorse for the person you hurt, what you did, and the pain you caused. The person or people affected by your behavior are not even there in this room with you, so their feelings and reactions must come from within you. You need to be able to convey genuine feelings of remorse to make amends successfully.

Ask for Forgiveness

When asking for forgiveness, you must be sincere. This means that you are willing to accept the consequences of your actions. You also need to be ready to make amends and change your behavior in the future. If someone has forgiven you and is willing to accept your apology but continues to treat you poorly or speak badly about you to others, it's okay not to go back into their lives right away—but do try again eventually. Forgiveness works both ways, and sometimes, even though a person says they forgive you, they might not be ready to mean it yet.

Ask What You Can Do to Amend Your Wrongdoing

While it may seem like a simple question, the "What can I do?" question is more of a two-part query: First, you're asking permission to make amends. Second, what they say after they tell you what they need from you determines whether or not your apology has been accepted.

This is an important part of making amends because it shows that you're taking ownership of your actions. It lets others know that you're not going to repeat the same mistakes repeatedly by offering them a way to avoid having to deal with your apologies every week or two.

Be Patient and Persistent

If you're looking to make amends with a loved one or family member, you must take the time to develop a plan. You'll also want to be mindful of your intention and follow through on it consistently over time.

It can sometimes feel like an uphill battle when trying not just to apologize but also to make amends for past mistakes. But remember: the most important thing is that you do what's best for yourself and your relationship with this person in the long run, even if it takes smaller steps at first. So don't be afraid of asking for help from others in AA who might have more experience in this area than you.

It's important to remember that making amends is a process. You can't expect everything to go perfectly when you try to do it for the first time but keep trying. And even though you might still make some mistakes along the way, don't let them discourage you from making amends in future situations where appropriate.

(A Self Awareness Model)

"Who Are You?"

_____

Name

_____

DEMOGRAPHIC

Hopefully by now, you have read Dr. Barbara Reddick's book, The Presence of a Chaplain & My Personal Tapestry of Life. If you have not, we encourage you to also read as well.

This section will allow you to look at self to become aware of who you are and who you may want to become. Please read each question carefully and explain in detail your thoughts, feelings, concerns, and observations.

Please understand that this is your personal tapestry of life and only you will read it unless you decide to share as I have. The journey in this student handbook will hopefully allow you to become empowered with your self-awareness. Work at your own pace, realizing that you can stop and start at any time.

(If you feel uncomfortable answering any of the questions, move on to the next question until you complete it. At the end of the journey, you may feel comfortable revisiting the unanswered questions.)

NAME:

DATE:

TIME:

AGE:

✓ EDUCATION

7th	8th	9th	10th	11th	12th	1 yr college	2 yr college	3 yr college	4 yr college	5 yr college	6 yr college

Male: _____

Female: _____

✓ Please (How many children do you have?)

- Married   Children: 1-2   3-4   5-6   7-8   9-10
- Divorce
- Single
- Dating
- Student

Share how you are feeling at this moment. (In detail)

_____

_____

_____

_____

_____

_____

_____

_____

_____

_____

_____

_____

_____

_____

_____

_____

_____

_____

_____

Do you have a clue of what you would like to learn about yourself?
YES _____   NO _____

Explain what you would like to learn about YOU?

_____

_____

_____

_____

_____

_____

_____

_____

_____

What is your favorite food? _____

What is your favorite game you like to play? _____

What do you like to do? _____

Who is your favorite Artist? _____

What grade are you presently in? _____

What is your favorite sport? _____

If you could meet a celebrity, who would you choose?_____

WHO RAISED YOU?

Mother Other Family	Father Uncle	Grandma Pastor	Grandpa Friends	Sister Neighbors	Brother Teacher	Auntie Cousin or Other

WHAT IS YOUR FAVORITE COLOR?

Do you have a pet, if so, share the name?

_____

_____

_____

_____

_____

_____

If you have a pet, describe the level of care you provide for your pet.

_____

_____

_____

How many pets have you had in your lifetime? _____

From a scale from 1 to 10, how would you number yourself as the level of care for pets? 1---don't care at all for pets   10--- care a whole lot

_____

Do you attend church? (Do not have to answer)
YES _____ NO ____

If you attend church, temple, or synagogue? What is your denomination?

_____

_____

_____

What do you like about your church, temple, or synagogue?

_____

_____

_____

What would You like to be when you grow up?

_____

_____

_____

How many siblings do you have? (circle)

1	2	3	4	5	6	7	8	9	10

How many stepsisters or step brothers do you have?

1	2	3	4	5	6	7	8	9	10

Do you like school? If no, explain why.

_____

_____

_____

_____

_____

_____

_____

_____

If you like school, explain in detail what you like about school and why?

_____

_____

_____

_____

_____

_____

_____

_____

While growing up who raised you? Explain this experience.

_____

_____

_____

_____

_____

_____

_____

_____

Are you okay with who raised you? If yes explain, if no explain.

_____

_____

_____

_____

_____

_____

_____

_____

How was your upbringing? Explain

_____

_____

_____

_____

_____

_____

_____

_____

_____

_____

_____

_____

_____

_____

_____

_____

_____

_____

Paint the picture in words how you would like for your family to look.

_____

_____

_____

_____

_____

_____

_____

_____

_____

If you could change one thing about your family lifestyle, what would it be?

_____
_____
_____

_____
_____
_____

_____
_____
_____

_____
_____

Are you being raised by both parents, single parent, or no parent, etc.?
Explain

_____
_____
_____
_____

_____
_____

_____
_____
_____

Which parent do you feel comfortable to share your deep thoughts with?
Mom _____ Dad ___ Other_____

Who is your favorite teacher and why?

_____
_____
_____

_____
_____
_____

_____
_____
_____

What is it you like about this teacher?

_____
_____
_____

If you could change one thing in your school, what would it be?

_____
_____
_____

_____
_____
_____

_____
_____
_____

Do you like your school that you are presently attending?

_____
_____
_____

If yes, why, if no why?

YES: _____

_____

_____

_____

_____

NO: _____

_____

_____

_____

_____

While growing up, did you spend time with grandma and grandpa?

_____

_____

_____

_____

_____

_____

_____

_____

If you spent time with either, explain how you felt then and now?

_____

_____

_____

_____

_____

_____

_____

_____

_____

If you did not spend time with your grandparents, how do you feel about this?

_____

_____

_____

_____

_____

_____

_____

_____

Do you feel that there are benefits for children who have grandparents in their lives? If so, why? If not, why?

_____

_____

_____

_____

_____

See how you are feeling NOW.

_____

_____

_____

_____

_____

Do you feel that this student handbook is helping you thus far?
YES _____ NO _____

Express how this student handbook is helping you thus far.

1.

_____
_____
_____
_____

2.

_____
_____
_____
_____

3.

_____
_____
_____
_____

What do you enjoy doing when you have free time?
_____
_____
_____

What are your strengths?
_____
_____
_____

What are your weaknesses?
_____
_____
_____

If you could change one thing about you, what would it be and why?

_____

_____

_____

_____

_____

_____

_____

_____

_____

If there is something you could change, do you feel that this has hindered you from moving forward in your life?

_____

_____

_____

_____

_____

_____

_____

_____

_____

_____

_____

_____

_____

_____

_____

_____

_____

Do you feel that life hasn't been fair?
YES _____ NO _____

EXPLAIN:

_____
_____
_____

_____
_____
_____

_____
_____
_____

_____
_____
_____

_____
_____
_____

_____
_____
_____

_____
_____
_____

If you feel that life for you hasn't been fair, identify one thing you can do to move things forward in a positive manner.

_____

_____

_____

_____

_____

_____

_____

_____

_____

Name one thing that you really dislike for someone to say or do to you?

_____

_____

_____

_____

_____

_____

_____

_____

Is there someone you are angry with?

If there is someone you are angry with, why?

_____

_____

_____

_____

_____

_____

Have you tried to resolve this matter?
YES _____ NO _____

Do you want to resolve the matter if it is not resolved currently? If yes, how do you plan on putting this behind you?

_____

_____

_____

_____

_____

_____

_____

_____

_____

ACTIVITY

TAKE TIME TO WRITE A LETTER TO SOME ONE
YOU WANT TO MAKE AMENDS WITH!
THERE MAY BE MORE THAN ONE PERSON.
USING THE NEXT FORMAT or YOU CAN USE YOUR PAPER.

FROM: _____
_____
_____

TO:_____
_____
_____

Dear _____:
_____
_____
_____

_____
_____
_____

_____
_____
_____

_____
_____
_____

_____ 52 _____
_____
_____
_____
_____
_____
_____
_____
_____
_____
_____
_____
_____
_____
_____
_____
_____

Sincerely,

TAKE A BREAK!!!!!!!
Debrief

Self-Care

Embrace the moment of your true feelings and know that if you are feeling angry, mad, happy, sad, or some anxiety, it's okay.

Examples of taking a break:

1. Take a walk!
2. Drink a cup of coffee or hot tea etc.
3. Inhale/Exhale
4. Yoga/Exercise
5. Meditation/Prayer
6. Self-Care

WELCOME BACK!!!!!!

TAKE AN OBSERVATION OF HOW YOU ARE FEELING AT THIS TIME.

_____

_____

_____

_____

_____

_____

_____

_____

_____

_____

_____

_____

_____

_____

_____

_____

_____

_____

External and Internal Alterations

Have you ever used drugs?
Yes _____ No _____

Have you ever used alcohol?
Yes _____ No _____

If yes, what type of drug have you ever used?

If not, explain on a separate sheet of paper, sharing a moment in your life where you wanted to use but didn't.

_____
_____
_____

_____
_____
_____

_____
_____
_____

_____
_____
_____

What kept you from using it?

_____

_____

_____

_____

_____

_____

Share this experience of how this make you feel that you were able to not use drugs or alcohol.

_____

_____

_____

_____

_____

_____

Cannabis _____ **Heroin** _____ **Cocaine** _____ **Crack Cocaine** ___
Hallucinogen _____ **Ecstasy** _____ **Methamphetamine**
_____**Molly**_____**Flakka**_____**Alcohol**_____

_____**Fentanyl**

Please explain the age you started using drugs. _____

Who introduced drugs to you? _____

How do you feel about this person today?

_____

_____

_____

_____

_____

_____

Did you trust this person at the time he or she introduced this drug to you?

_____
_____
_____

_____
_____
_____

_____
_____
_____

_____
_____
_____

What would you do differently if you could turn back the hands of time?

_____
_____
_____

_____
_____
_____

_____
_____
_____

_____
_____
_____

How do you feel about leaders?

_____

_____

_____

_____

_____

_____

_____

_____

How do you feel a leader should lead?

_____

_____

_____

_____

_____

_____

_____

_____

_____

_____

_____

_____

If you attend church, temple, or synagogue, how do you feel about your pastor, rabbi, or priest, etc.?

_____

_____

_____

_____

_____

_____

_____

_____

_____

_____

Does your pastor, rabbi, priest, etc., exemplify good leadership skills?

_____

_____

_____

_____

_____

_____

_____

_____

_____

_____

If not, identify the areas you would like your leader to improve in.

_____

_____

_____

_____

_____

_____

_____

_____

_____

Define leadership.

_____

_____

_____

_____

_____

_____

_____

_____

_____

_____

_____

_____

How do you feel about this overall observation of self and others?

_____

_____

_____

_____

_____

_____

_____

_____

_____

_____

_____

_____

_____

_____

_____

Would you recommend this workbook to someone else?
Yes _____   **No** _____

GREAT WORK!!! YOU DESERVE A PAT ON THE BACK. I look forward to speaking with you soon. We can arrange for a conference call if you'd like.

Dr. Barbara Thomas-Reddick

WHEN YOU DO NOT KNOW WHO YOU ARE, YOU WILL BE WHAT OTHERS WANT YOU TO BE!!!

"WHO ARE YOU?"

_____

_____

_____

WHEN YOU COMPLETE YOUR HANDBOOK, IN ORDER TO RECEIVE YOUR CERTIFICATE OF COMPLETION, CONTACT Dr. Barbara Thomas-Reddick at 850-201-7105 Office/ 850-201-7101 Fax or email me at Holisticplanofcare@gmail.com

IF YOU WOULD LIKE TO BOOK DR. BARBARA THOMAS- REDDICK FOR FUTURE ENGAGEMENTS FEEL FREE TO CONTACT ME AT THE NUMBER ABOVE.

WEBSITE:
www.thepresenceofachaplain.com
WWW.HPOCARE.ORG
www.ifgoddontdoit.com

Stay focused for upcoming book on PARENTING.

LET'S TAKE A POST ANGER TEST AND COMPARE THE TWO.

(POST) TESTING YOUR ANGER CONTROL

1. I get angry with little or no provocation.
   1   2   3   4   5

2. I have a really bad temper.
   1   2   3   4   5

3. It's hard for me to let go of thoughts that make me angry.
   1   2   3   4   5

4. When I become angry, I have urges to beat someone up.
   1   2   3   4   5

5. When I become angry, I have urges to break or tear things.
   1   2   3   4   5

6. I get impatient when people don't understand me.
   1   2   3   4   5

7. I lose my temper at least once a week.
   1   2   3   4   5

8. I embarrass family, friends, or coworkers with my anger outbursts.
   1   2   3   4   5

9. I get impatient when people in front of me drive *exactly at* the speed limit.
   1   2   3   4   5

10. When my neighbors are inconsiderate, it makes me angry.
    1   2   3   4   5

11. I find myself frequently annoyed with certain friends or family.
    1   2   3   4   5

12. I get angry when people do things that they are not supposed to, like smoking in a no smoking section or having more items than marked in the supermarket express checkout line.

    1   2   3   4   5

13. There are certain people who always rub me the wrong way.

    1   2   3   4   5

14. I feel uptight/tense.

    1   2   3   4   5

15. I yell and/or curse.

    1   2   3   4   5

16. I get so angry I feel like I am going to explode with rage.

    1   2   3   4   5

17. I get easily frustrated when machines/equipment do not work properly

    1   2   3   4   5

18. I remember people and situations that made me angry for a long time.

    1   2   3   4   5

19. I can't tolerate incompetence. It makes me angry.

    1   2   3   4   5

20. I think people try to take advantage of me.

    1   2   3   4   5

TOTAL: _____

Score Key:

80-100 Your anger expression is likely getting you into serious trouble with others. It would probably be worthwhile to seek professional help.

60-80 You may not need professional help but you need to work on controlling your anger in a very deliberate manner.

50-60 You have plenty of room for improvement. Reading a self-help book on anger control could be beneficial.

30-50 You're probably getting angry as often as most people. Monitor your episodes of temper and see if you can lower your score in this test in 6 months.

Below 30- Congratulate yourself. You are likely in a good comfort zone.

Final Test for completion

1. **Who is the Professor for this class?**
   a. **Joyce Melanie**
   b. **Dr. Roy Lee**
   c. **Dr. Barbara Thomas-Reddick**

2. **Define Anger**
   a. **a strong feeling of annoyance, displeasure, or hostility**
   b. **Anger can be a good thing. It can give you a way to express negative feelings, for example, or motivate you to find solutions to problems.**
   c. **It is okay to be angry, it is what you do with it.**
   d. **All above**

3. **Write down the three types of Anger?**
   1. _____
   2. _____
   3. _____

4. **Learning to recognize and express anger appropriately can make a bid difference in your life.**
   True or False (circle)

5. **The Five Stages of Anger.**
   a. _____   b. _____
   c. _____   d. _____
   e. _____

6. **Mental health includes our:**
   a. **emotional well-being**
   b. **psychological well-being**
   c. **social well-being**
   d. **ALL OF THE ABOVE**

7. Mental health is important at
    a. the end of live
    b. at every state of live
    c. at the beginning of the situation
    d. ALL OF THE ABOVE

8. Mental health is important because it can help you to:
    a. Cope with the stresses of live
    b. Seek more jobs to do
    c. Have a good relationship
    d. Be physically healthy
    e. Make meaningful contributions to your community
    f. a, c, d, e

9. Mental health affects how we:
    a. think, feel and act
    b. how we attend church
    c. what job we choose

10. From a scale from 1-10, (1 being not so good, 10 being doing great), how would you rate your mental status at this time? _____

AFTER YOU HAVE COMPLETED THE CLASS WITH A 70% or higher, YOU WILL RECEIVE A CERTIFICATE OF COMPLETION IN YOUR EMAIL. SIGNED BY Dr. Barbara Thomas-Reddick or another Holistic Plan of Care Member. (HPOC)

HOLISTIC PLAN OF CARE, INCORPORATED

N A M E

S HERE NOW RECOGNIZED FOR SUCESSFUL COMPLETION

Of the

MENTAL HEALTH CLASS

On

DATE

_____

CEO/FACILITATOR/Certified Addiction Professional

NOTES:

Printed in the United States
by Baker & Taylor Publisher Services